CRISTIANO
RONALDO
THE ELITE MENTALITY
AF479508

Table of Contents

CHAPTER 1:
The Boy from Funchal

Before the cameras captured his every move, before the stadiums of the world shook with the deafening roar of *"Siuuu!"*, and before he became a global icon, Cristiano Ronaldo dos Santos Aveiro was just a skinny boy with messy hair and an unbreakable spirit. He was born on February 5, 1985, on the rugged, volcanic island of Madeira, Portugal.

Funchal, the island's capital, is a city built on steep hillsides that plunge toward the Atlantic Ocean. For most people, these hills were just part of the landscape. For young Cristiano, they were his first training ground. He grew up in the San Antonio neighborhood, living in a small, tin-roofed house where space was tight and money was even tighter. His father, José Dinis Aveiro, worked as a municipal gardener, and his mother, Maria Dolores, worked as a cook and cleaning lady. Together, they worked tirelessly to provide for Cristiano and his three older siblings: Hugo, Elma, and Katia.

DID YOU KNOW? Cristiano's full name is Cristiano Ronaldo dos Santos Aveiro. He was named "Ronaldo" after his father's favorite American actor, Ronald Reagan.

While the Aveiro family didn't have much in the way of luxury, their home was filled with energy. Much like the streets of Rocafonda or Rosario, the air in Funchal was often filled with a familiar sound: the rhythmic *thump-thump-thump* of a ball hitting a wall. From the moment Cristiano could walk, he was drawn to the ball. His family often tells stories of how he would dribble through the small rooms of their home, practicing his turns around chairs and table legs as if they were world-class defenders.

Cristiano didn't just play football; he *needed* it. If he didn't have a real ball, he would make one out of rags or old socks tied together. He was a child who lived for the challenge. In his neighborhood, football was woven into the fabric of everyday life. Games would break out in the middle of narrow streets, on dusty empty lots, and on steep sidewalks where one wrong move could send the ball rolling hundreds of feet down the hill.

Even at five or six years old, people began to notice that this quiet boy moved differently. While other kids chased the ball in a big, messy pack, Cristiano seemed to have a map of the pitch in his head. He understood where the ball was going before it even got there. He found spaces others couldn't see and played with a level of focus that made him stand out. For Cristiano, football wasn't just a sport—it was a language he already understood fluently.

As a young boy, he was nicknamed "Abelinha" (Little Bee) because he never stopped moving. He was always buzzing around the field, looking for a way to score, a way to win, and a way to improve. This relentless energy and refusal to be outworked would become the foundation of his legendary career.

CHAPTER 2:
The School of the Streets

In most parts of the world, schools have desks, chalkboards, and teachers. But for Cristiano Ronaldo, his most important school didn't have a roof. It was the Quinta do Falcão, the steep, rugged neighborhood where he spent every waking hour after his formal classes ended.

If you look at a map of Funchal, you will see that the streets aren't flat like a professional football pitch. They are tilted, winding, and often made of rough asphalt or cobblestone. This was Cristiano's "classroom."

The Asphalt Advantage

Playing on the hills of Madeira was a lesson in physics and survival. If the ball went over a fence, you had to climb for it. If the ball rolled down the hill, you had to sprint to catch it before it reached the bottom. Because the ground was uneven, the ball would bounce in unpredictable ways.

While this might sound difficult, it gave Cristiano three "Superpowers" that he still uses today:

1. **Balance:** To keep from falling on the steep slopes, Cristiano developed a very strong "core." This is why, even today, it is very hard for defenders to knock him off the ball.

2. **Fast Reflexes:** On the street, the ball doesn't roll smoothly. You have to react in a split second to a weird bounce. This turned Cristiano into a "reactive" player who could move faster than anyone else.

3. **The Step-Over:** Because he was often smaller and skinnier than the older boys in the neighborhood, Cristiano couldn't use his strength to win. He had to use his feet to trick them. He practiced his "step-overs"—moving his feet over the ball without touching it—thousands of times until his legs moved like a blur.

"The Boy Who Never Came In"

His mother, Dolores, often tells the story that when she called Cristiano for dinner, he would pretend not to hear her. He would stay outside until it was so dark he could barely see the ball. Sometimes, he didn't even have a real ball; he would use a plastic bottle or a bundle of rags.

Just like Lamine Yamal playing in the parks of Rocafonda or Messi on the dirt lots of Grandoli, Cristiano learned that you don't need a fancy stadium to become a legend. You just need a ball and a "never-give-up" attitude.

The Hardest Lesson: "The Wall"

In Quinta do Falcão, there were no fancy training cones. Cristiano used the walls of the neighborhood buildings. He would kick the ball against the wall with his right foot, catch the rebound, and immediately kick it with his left. He did this until he was "two-footed," meaning he could shoot just as well with his left foot as his right. Most professional players struggle to do this, but Cristiano mastered it before he was ten years old!

COACH'S CORNER: WHY STREET FOOTBALL IS BETTER THAN A ACADEMY

- Creativity: There are no coaches telling you what to do. You have to figure out how to score on your own.

- Toughness: If you fall on asphalt, it hurts. You learn to be "street-smart" and physically brave.

- Freedom: You can try new tricks without being afraid of making a mistake.

CHAPTER 3:
The First Club and the "Crybaby"

By the time Cristiano was seven years old, his talent was too big for the streets of Funchal to contain. His father, Dinis, worked as the kit man for a small local club called Andorinha. A kit man is the person responsible for looking after the jerseys, shorts, and equipment for the team. Because Dinis was always at the club, Cristiano was always there too.

Joining Andorinha was Cristiano's first taste of "real" football—with referees, jerseys, and a grass pitch. But there was a problem: the other kids were older, bigger, and stronger. To Cristiano, that didn't matter. He played with a fierce intensity that actually scared some of the other children. He would sprint until his lungs burned, and he expected everyone else to do the same.

It was during these years at Andorinha that Cristiano earned a nickname that followed him for a long time: "Abelinha" (Little Bee). He was called this because he never stopped "buzzing" around the field. He was everywhere at once—defending, passing, and scoring.

However, there was another nickname that his teammates used when he wasn't listening: "Crybaby."

THE STORY BEHIND THE NICKNAME Cristiano didn't cry because he was hurt or because he was bullied. He cried because of his passion. If he passed the ball to a teammate and they missed the goal, Cristiano would burst into tears. If his team lost a game, he would sob on the grass. He couldn't understand how anyone could be okay with losing. Even as a child, his standards were impossibly high.

This "Crybaby" phase was actually the first sign of what coaches call Elite Mentality. While other kids went home and forgot about a loss, Cristiano stayed awake thinking about what he could do better. He was learning that to be the best, you have to care more than everyone else.

At age ten, the biggest club on the island, Nacional, came calling. They had heard rumors of a boy at Andorinha who could dribble through entire teams. To sign him, Nacional didn't pay millions of dollars. Instead, they reportedly traded a set of football kits and boots to Andorinha in exchange for the young prodigy.

At Nacional, the stakes got higher. Cristiano was no longer just the best kid in the neighborhood; he was the best kid on the island. He began to realize that his feet could take him places his family had never been. But to get there, he would have to face a challenge much bigger than a lost game. He would have to leave his home behind.

THE VOCABULARY OF A CHAMPION

- Kit Man: The person who manages a team's uniforms and gear.

- Prodigy: A young person with exceptional qualities or abilities.

- Elite Mentality: A mindset focused on constant improvement and a refusal to accept failure.

- Trade: When a team exchanges players or items instead of using money.

CHAPTER 4:
Leaving the Island

In 1997, a life-changing piece of paper arrived in Funchal. It was a contract from Sporting CP, one of the "Big Three" clubs in Portugal. They had seen Cristiano play for Nacional and were convinced he was the greatest talent they had ever seen on the islands.

But there was a catch. Sporting CP's academy was in Lisbon, the capital city of Portugal. Lisbon was on the mainland, hundreds of miles across the Atlantic Ocean. For 12-year-old Cristiano, it might as well have been on the moon.

The Hardest Goodbye

Imagine being 12 years old. You have never lived anywhere but your small neighborhood. You have never been away from your mother's cooking, your brother's jokes, or the familiar smell of the sea.

The day Cristiano had to leave was the saddest day of his life. His mother, Dolores, walked him to the airport. They were both crying so hard they could barely speak. Cristiano was terrified, but he knew this was his only chance to help his family escape poverty. He boarded the plane with nothing but a small suitcase and a heart full of nerves.

A Stranger in His Own Country

When Cristiano arrived at the Sporting academy, things didn't get easier. Even though he was in Portugal, the people in Lisbon spoke with a different accent than the people in Madeira.

On his first day of school, when Cristiano stood up to introduce himself, the other students started laughing. To them, he sounded "foreign" or "country-like." Cristiano was a proud boy, and being mocked made him feel small. He felt like an outsider in his own country.

He spent his first few months in Lisbon crying every night. He would call his mother from a payphone, begging to come home. But Dolores, showing the same strength her son would later show on the pitch, told him: *"Don't give up. You are there for a reason."*

The Training Ground Refuge

The only time Cristiano felt happy was on the training pitch. The moment he laced up his boots, the teasing stopped. The boys who laughed at his accent in the classroom were suddenly silent when he had the ball at his feet.

He was faster than the older boys. He was more skillful than the captains. He began to realize that while he couldn't control how people talked about him, he could control how they felt about his football. He decided right then that if he couldn't fit in, he would stand out.

The Academy Mindset

At the Sporting academy, Cristiano learned that talent is only 50% of the puzzle. The other 50% is discipline. He saw that the players who made it to the professional level weren't always the ones with the best tricks—they were the ones who showed up first and stayed last.

The Secret Gym Sessions

Cristiano was still very skinny, and the coaches told him he needed to get stronger if he wanted to play with the adults. Because he wasn't allowed in the gym late at night, Cristiano would wait until the coaches were asleep. He would sneak out of his dorm, go to the gym, and lift weights in the dark.

One night, a coach caught him. Instead of being angry, the coach was amazed. He realized that this boy from Madeira had a "fire" inside him that couldn't be put out.

GEOGRAPHY BOX: PORTUGAL'S FOOTBALL HUB

- Madeira: A small island known for its beauty, but isolated from the big football leagues.

- Lisbon: The capital city and the home of world-class scouts and training facilities.

- The Mainland: In Portugal, people call the main part of the country "The Continent." Moving there is considered a huge step up for any athlete.

CHAPTER 5:
The Professional Debut

By the time Cristiano turned sixteen, the coaches at Sporting CP realized they weren't looking at a normal academy player. They were looking at a phenomenon. Most young players move through the ranks one step at a time: Under-16, then Under-17, then the B-team, and finally the first team. Cristiano did something that had never been done in the history of the club. In a single season, he played for the U16, U17, U18, the B-team, and the senior professional team.

He was moving at light speed, but his debut was the moment the world finally got to see the "Madeira Magic" on a big stage.

The Big Night in Lisbon

On October 7, 2002, seventeen-year-old Cristiano walked into the locker room of the Estádio José Alvalade. He looked at the professional jerseys hanging on the hooks. For years, he had been the boy who sneaked into the gym and cried in the phone booths. Now, he was wearing the green and white horizontal stripes of the Sporting first team in a league match against Moreirense.

When he stepped onto the pitch, the atmosphere was electric. He didn't look nervous; he looked hungry. In the 34th minute, it happened. Cristiano received the ball near the center circle. Instead of passing, he put his head down and began a trademark run.

He skipped past one defender, stepped over the ball to confuse a second, and then used his blistering speed to leave the third in the dust. As the goalkeeper came out, Cristiano calmly slotted the ball into the net. He didn't just score; he later scored a second goal in the same game with a powerful header. The stadium erupted. The "Crybaby" was gone—the "Pro" had arrived.

The Scout's Notebook

While the fans were cheering, there were men in the stands wearing long coats and holding notebooks. These were scouts from the biggest clubs in Europe: Juventus, Barcelona, and Arsenal. They were all writing the same thing: *"Sign this kid immediately."*

Arsène Wenger, the famous manager of Arsenal, actually invited Cristiano to London. Cristiano even wore an Arsenal jersey and met with the team. It seemed certain he would move to London. But destiny had a different plan, and it involved a friendly match that would change the course of football history forever.

CHAPTER 6:
The Game That Changed Everything

In August 2003, Sporting CP organized a friendly match to inaugurate their brand-new stadium. Their opponents? The most famous team in the world: Manchester United.

Manchester United was coached by the legendary Sir Alex Ferguson. They had stars like Paul Scholes, Ryan Giggs, and Rio Ferdinand. They expected a nice, easy practice game before their season started. They didn't realize they were about to walk into a hurricane named Cristiano.

Dizzied Defenders

From the first whistle, Cristiano targeted United's right-back, John O'Shea. He was performing step-overs, "rabonas," and "flicks" that the United players had never seen before. He was so fast that O'Shea reportedly needed an oxygen tank at halftime because he was so exhausted from chasing the teenager!

In the locker room at halftime, the Manchester United players weren't talking about their own tactics. They were talking about the skinny kid with the blonde highlights in his hair.

Inside The Locker Room

Rio Ferdinand, one of the world's best defenders, recalled: "We were sitting there saying to the manager, 'Boss, we have to sign him. He's amazing. We can't leave without him.'"

The Secret Meeting

Sir Alex Ferguson didn't need much convincing. He was a man who knew greatness when he saw it. After the game, while the other Sporting players were celebrating their 3-1 victory, Ferguson refused to let the Manchester United bus leave the stadium.

He sent for Cristiano. In a small room deep inside the stadium, the most powerful manager in football looked at the eighteen-year-old boy from Madeira and said, *"I want you to come to Manchester. And I want you to play for me."*

Less than a week later, Cristiano was on a private jet. He thought he would stay in Portugal for one more year on loan. But Ferguson told him, *"No. You are coming with me now. You are ready."*

THE SCOUT'S GLOSSARY: TERMS OF THE TRADE

- Debut: A player's first appearance in a professional game.

- Senior Team: The top-level professional squad, above the youth academies.

- Friendly Match: A game played for practice or exhibition, where the result doesn't count toward league standings.

- Loan: When a player is "borrowed" by another team for a season to get more experience.

CHAPTER 7:
The Theater of Dreams

When Cristiano stepped off the plane in England in August 2003, he wasn't just a new player—he was a piece of history. At just eighteen years old, he became the first-ever Portuguese player to sign for Manchester United. The club paid £12.24 million for him, which was a record-breaking fee for a teenager at the time.

But it wasn't the money that people were talking about. It was the number on his back.

The Magic of Number 7

In the world of Manchester United, the number 7 jersey is legendary. It has been worn by some of the greatest players to ever touch a football, like George Best, Eric Cantona, and David Beckham.

Cristiano originally asked for the number 28 (the number he wore at Sporting), because he was afraid of the pressure of the famous #7. But Sir Alex Ferguson looked him in the eye and said, *"No. You are wearing the seven. You are going to be one of the greats."*

DID YOU KNOW? The nickname "CR7" was born at Manchester United. It combines his initials (Cristiano Ronaldo) and his shirt number (7). Today, it is one of the most famous brand names in the world!

The Debut That Dazzled

Cristiano didn't have to wait long to show the English fans what he could do. On August 16, 2003, he came off the bench as a substitute against Bolton Wanderers. The score was 1-0, and the game was tense.

The moment he stepped onto the grass at Old Trafford—known as the "Theater of Dreams"—the energy shifted. He began to do things the English fans had never seen. He was doing multiple step-overs at high speed, "no-look" passes, and crossing the ball with pinpoint accuracy. By the time the final whistle blew, United had won 4-0, and the fans were singing his name.

Hard Work Behind the Scenes

While the fans saw the magic on Saturdays, his teammates saw the "grind" every other day of the week. Cristiano was never satisfied with being "good." He wanted to be "the best in history."

His former teammate Rio Ferdinand tells a story about how Cristiano hired a personal chef, a personal physiotherapist, and even a personal sleep coach. This was unheard of in 2004! While other players went home to play video games after practice, Cristiano stayed on the field. He would tie weights to his ankles and practice his dribbling to make his feet faster. He would stay out in the rain practicing "knuckleball" free kicks until the sun went down.

CHAPTER 8:
The Best in the World (2008)

If his first few years in Manchester were about learning, the year 2008 was about conquering. This was the year Cristiano Ronaldo officially became the king of football.

The Perfect Season

In the 2007–08 season, Cristiano was unstoppable. He wasn't just a winger anymore; he was a goal-scoring machine. He scored a staggering 42 goals in all competitions. For a player who wasn't even a traditional striker, this was almost impossible.

He helped Manchester United win the Premier League title, but the biggest prize was still to come: the UEFA Champions League.

The Rainy Night in Moscow

The 2008 Champions League Final was an all-English battle between Manchester United and Chelsea, held in a rainy Moscow stadium. Cristiano scored a brilliant header to put United in the lead, but the game eventually went to a penalty shootout.

In a dramatic turn of events, Cristiano actually *missed* his penalty during the shootout. He was devastated, thinking he had cost his team the trophy. He lay facedown in the grass, crying in the pouring rain. But when Chelsea's captain slipped and missed his own shot, United seized the chance and won!

Cristiano went from heartbreak to pure joy in seconds. He had won the biggest trophy in club football.

The Ballon d'Or

Because of his incredible performance that year, Cristiano was awarded his very first Ballon d'Or—the trophy given to the single best player on the planet. He was only 23 years old.

At that moment, he had reached the top of the mountain. He had fulfilled the promise he made to his mother back on the island of Madeira. He was the best in the world. But Cristiano wasn't done. He had a new dream: he wanted to play for the "White House" of football—Real Madrid.

- Old Trafford: The home stadium of Manchester United, nicknamed the "Theater of Dreams."

- Winger: A player who plays near the sides of the field, usually very fast and good at crossing the ball.

- Ballon d'Or: French for "Golden Ball." It is the most prestigious individual award in football.

- Knuckleball: A way of kicking the ball that makes it wobble and dip in the air, making it very hard for goalkeepers to catch.

CHAPTER 9:
The World Record Transfer

In the summer of 2009, the football world was shaken by a single announcement. Real Madrid, the most successful club in history, had signed Cristiano Ronaldo for a staggering £80 million (about $131 million). At the time, it was the most expensive transfer in history.

The "Boy from Funchal" was no longer just a star—il was a "Galáctico" (a superstar).

The Presentation

On July 6, 2009, 80,000 fans packed into the Santiago Bernabéu Stadium just to see Cristiano walk onto the pitch in a white jersey. This broke a 25-year-old record for the most-attended player presentation, which was previously held by Diego Maradona.

Cristiano stepped onto the stage, looked at the sea of fans, and famously shouted, *"Uno, dos, tres... ¡Hala Madrid!"* The stadium erupted. He was given the number 9 jersey because the legendary Raul was still wearing the number 7, but the world knew it was only a matter of time before CR7 returned.

The "Machine" in Madrid

At Real Madrid, Cristiano transformed from a flashy winger into the most efficient goal-scoring machine the game had ever seen. He realized that to dominate the Spanish league (La Liga), he had to change his style. He became stronger, faster, and more focused on the final touch.

- **Training Secrets:** He reportedly arrived at the training ground two hours before everyone else and left two hours after.

- **The Diet:** He famously eats six small meals a day, focusing on fish, chicken, and fresh vegetables. He drinks only water—never soda!

- **The Recovery:** He installed a "cryotherapy" chamber in his house, which uses freezing temperatures to help his muscles recover after games.

CHAPTER 10:
The Greatest Rivalry

For the next nine years, football fans were treated to the greatest individual rivalry in sports history. Every weekend, it was a battle: If Lionel Messi scored a hat-trick for Barcelona on Saturday, Cristiano Ronaldo would score four goals for Real Madrid on Sunday.

They were like two superheroes from different universes.

- Messi was the "Natural Genius"—small, quiet, and magical with the ball "glued" to his feet.

- Ronaldo was the "Ultimate Athlete"—tall, powerful, and a product of thousands of hours of hard work and discipline.

DID YOU KNOW? Between 2008 and 2017, only two men won the Ballon d'Or: Messi and Ronaldo. They shared the stage for a decade, pushing each other to be better every single day.

This rivalry didn't just make them famous; it made them better. Cristiano once said that playing in the same league as Messi gave him the "hunger" to keep winning. They weren't just playing against each other; they were playing against history.

WORD POWER: THE LANGUAGE OF LA LIGA

- Galáctico: A Spanish term for a superstar player signed by Real Madrid.

- Hat-trick: When a player scores three goals in a single game.

- El Clásico: The famous match between Real Madrid and FC Barcelona—the biggest game in club football.

- Cryotherapy: Using cold temperatures to help athletes recover from injuries and fatigue.

CHAPTER 11:
The King of Europe

If the Champions League is the most difficult tournament in the world, then Cristiano Ronaldo is its undisputed king. During his time at Real Madrid, he didn't just win the trophy—he owned it. Between 2014 and 2018, Cristiano led Real Madrid to four Champions League titles, including three in a row, a feat many thought was impossible in the modern era.

2014: La Décima (The Tenth)

For twelve years, Real Madrid fans had been waiting for their tenth European title, known in Spain as *La Décima*. In 2014, the final was held in Lisbon—the city where Cristiano had struggled as a lonely twelve-year-old.

It was a dramatic "Derby" against their rivals, Atlético Madrid. Real was losing until the very last minute of the game! After a miracle equalizer by Sergio Ramos, the game went into extra time. Cristiano scored a penalty to seal a 4-1 victory. He celebrated by ripping off his jersey and showing the world the muscles he had worked so hard to build in the dark gyms of Lisbon. He had brought the trophy back to Madrid.

2016 & 2017: Back-to-Back Greatness

In 2016, the final once again went to a penalty shootout. As the team's leader, Cristiano stepped up for the final, deciding kick. The pressure was immense, but he remained calm, slotted the ball home, and won his third title.

In 2017, Real Madrid faced the Italian giants, Juventus. Cristiano was unstoppable, scoring two goals in a 4-1 win. With this victory, Real Madrid became the first team in history to win the Champions League back-to-back since the tournament was renamed in 1992.

2018: The "Impossible" Goal

While Cristiano won his fifth total Champions League title in 2018 (beating Liverpool 3-1), the moment everyone remembers happened in the quarter-final against Juventus.

Cristiano leaped into the air—nearly eight feet high—and performed a perfect bicycle kick. He struck the ball so cleanly that even the opposing fans in Italy stood up and cheered for him. It is widely considered the greatest goal in the history of the competition.

CHAPTER 12:
Glory with Portugal

For many years, critics said, *"Cristiano is great for his clubs, but he never wins anything for his country."* In 2016, he set out to prove them wrong at the UEFA European Championship (Euro 2016).

The Captain's Sacrifice

Portugal wasn't the favorite to win. They were the underdogs. But Cristiano dragged his team to the final against France. However, early in the final match, Cristiano suffered a painful knee injury. He tried to play through the pain, but eventually, he had to be carried off the field on a stretcher, tears streaming down his face.

But he didn't go to the locker room. He came back out to the sideline with a bandage on his knee. He spent the rest of the game acting like a second coach, screaming instructions and motivating his teammates. When Portugal scored the winning goal in extra time, Cristiano jumped for joy, forgetting all about his injury. He had finally won a major trophy for his beloved Portugal.

THE CHAMPION'S STAT BOARD: THE UCL
RECORDS

- Most Goals: 140+ (The all-time leader)

- Most Goals in a Single Season: 17 (2013-14)

- Most Titles: 5 (1 with Man Utd, 4 with Real
  Madrid)

- First Player to Score in 3 Different Finals

CHAPTER 13:
Italy and the Return Home

A New Challenge in Italy

Imagine conquering the highest mountain in the world, not once, but four times. For most people, reaching the absolute top is enough. But Cristiano Ronaldo is always looking for the next peak. In 2018, after winning an incredible four Champions League titles in Madrid, Cristiano decided he needed a brand new challenge. He packed his bags and moved to Italy to join the legendary club, Juventus.

Italian football is famous for having some of the toughest and smartest defenders in the world. Many thought Cristiano would finally struggle. After all, he was in his mid-30s. In the world of professional football, that is the age when most players start to slow down and lose their explosive energy. But Cristiano defied the odds and was as fast as ever.

He dominated the pitch, helping Juventus win two Serie A titles. He even shattered records by becoming the fastest player in the club's entire history to score 100 goals. His incredible physical condition left everyone in awe. In Italy, they even nicknamed him "The Cyborg" because his body seemed like a high-tech machine that was absolutely impossible to break.

The Homecoming

Just when fans thought Cristiano might settle down in Italy, the football world was shocked again in 2021. Cristiano made the emotional decision to return to where his

incredible journey into superstardom first began:
Manchester United.

The atmosphere at Old Trafford was pure magic. The fans
cried tears of joy to finally see their ultimate hero back
home, proudly wearing his famous #7 jersey once again.

But the biggest question remained: could he still perform in
the fast-paced English league? He answered that question
immediately. In his very first game back with the Red
Devils, Cristiano scored two spectacular goals. He proved
to the entire world that even though he was older, his sharp
"killer instinct" in front of the net hadn't changed at all. The
king had returned, and he was as hungry for victory as ever.

CHAPTER 14:
The Road to 1,000

In 2023, Cristiano made a move that changed the map of world football. He signed for Al-Nassr in Saudi Arabia. Many people thought he was going there to retire, but they were wrong.

Cristiano didn't go to Saudi Arabia to relax; he went to win. He became the league's top scorer, often scoring hat-tricks that left fans breathless. His move was so big that other superstars like Neymar and Karim Benzema followed him to the desert.

The Ultimate Goal: 1,000

As we stand here in early 2026, Cristiano is chasing a number that no professional male player in history has ever officially reached: 1,000 career goals.

As of January 2026, he has already crossed 950 goals! At age 40 (soon to be 41), he is still the captain of Portugal and Al-Nassr. He has told the world that he wants to play in the 2026 World Cup in North America. Imagine—a boy from a tiny island playing in his sixth World Cup!

CRISTIANO'S 2026 MISSION: "I don't follow the records," Cristiano famously said. "The records follow me." His goal for 2026 is simple: Stay fit, help Portugal win, and hit that magical 1,000th goal.

CHAPTER 15:
The Legend of CR7

So, what makes Cristiano Ronaldo different from everyone else? Is it his speed? His jumping ability? His powerful "knuckleball" free kicks? While those physical skills are undeniably world-class, the true secret to his success is actually something you can't see on a TV screen: His Mind.

Long before the sold-out stadiums, the record-breaking transfers, and the millions of chanting fans, Cristiano was just a kid with a football and a dream. Cristiano's story is a message to every kid who has ever been told they are "too skinny," "too poor," or "too far away." He didn't let the rough, uneven streets of Madeira or the lonely, difficult nights in Lisbon stop him from chasing his ultimate goals. Instead, he used those exact challenges as his fuel. He showed us that where you start doesn't define where you finish.

When he was laughed at, he let his footwork do the talking. When he was knocked down by bigger defenders, he got back up and ran faster. He turned his tears into trophies and his "Crybaby" nickname into a symbol of the greatest winner the game has ever seen. True legends aren't simply born; they are built through thousands of hours of unseen hard work, an unwavering belief in themselves, and an elite mentality that refuses to ever accept defeat.

THE CR7 GLOSSARY

- Serie A: The top professional football league in Italy.

- Cyborg: A nickname given to Ronaldo because of his incredible physical fitness and health.

- Al-Nassr: The club in Riyadh, Saudi Arabia, where Cristiano currently plays.

- Legacy: The impact and memory a person leaves behind for future generations.

CHAPTER 16:
Training Like a Titan

If you want to play like Ronaldo, you have to live like Ronaldo. He views his body as a high-performance sports car—and you wouldn't put cheap fuel or bad tires on a Ferrari, would you?

The "Secret" Daily Schedule

Cristiano's day is built around consistency. He doesn't just train when he feels like it; he follows a strict ritual:

1. The Morning Wake-up: He starts with a high-protein breakfast (cheese, ham, and low-fat yogurt).

2. Five Naps: Instead of sleeping eight hours straight at night, Cristiano often takes five 90-minute naps throughout the day. This keeps his brain and muscles fresh.

3. Water Only: You will never see Cristiano drinking soda. In a famous moment at a press conference, he moved two bottles of Coca-Cola away and held up a water bottle, shouting, *"Agua!"* 4. The Gym Routine: He focuses on "explosive" movements— things that help him jump high and sprint fast. He often does 1,000+ ab crunches in a single week to keep his core rock-solid.

Recovery is Key

The reason Cristiano is still playing in 2026 at the age of 41 is because of how he recovers.

- Ice Baths: After every game, he sits in a tub of ice-cold water to reduce swelling.

- No Tattoos: Have you noticed Cristiano doesn't have any tattoos? He chooses not to get them so he can donate blood and bone marrow more frequently to help sick children.

FUN FACTS: Things You Didn't Know!

- Named after a President: His father's favorite actor was Ronald Reagan (who was also the U.S. President), so he named his son "Ronaldo."

- The "Little Bee": When he was a kid, his friends called him "Abelinha" (Little Bee) because he never stopped buzzing around the pitch.

- He Can Outjump a Basketball Player: In one game, Cristiano jumped so high that his head was 2.93 meters (9.6 feet) off the ground. That's higher than the average NBA player's jump!

- Museum of Me: Cristiano has his very own museum in his hometown of Funchal, Madeira. It's called Museu CR7, and it holds all his trophies and medals.

- Social Media King: Cristiano was the first person in history to reach 600 million followers on Instagram. He has more fans online than the entire population of North America!

THE RONALDO QUIZ: Are You A Cr7 Superfan?

1. On what date was Cristiano Ronaldo born?

A) February 5, 1985

B) October 7, 1985

C) July 6, 1984

D) August 16, 1986

2. Which Portuguese island is Cristiano Ronaldo originally from?

A) Azores

B) Madeira

C) Porto Santo

D) Cape Verde

3. What was his father's profession at the local municipality?

A) Street sweeper

B) Bus driver

C) Gardener

D) Electrician

4. Who was Cristiano named after?

A) His grandfather

B) A famous Portuguese poet

C) The American actor and President Ronald Reagan

D) A Brazilian football legend

5. What was Cristiano's childhood nickname because he never stopped moving on the pitch?

A) El Rápido (The Fast One)

B) Andorinha (The Swallow)

C) Abelinha (Little Bee)

D) El Viento (The Wind)

6. What was the name of Cristiano's first organized football club?

A) Nacional

B) Andorinha

C) Sporting CP

D) Marítimo

7. Why did his childhood teammates sometimes call him "Crybaby"?

A) He cried when the older boys tackled him too hard.

B) He cried when he had to go home for dinner.

C) He cried out of passion if his team lost or a teammate missed a goal.

D) He cried because he missed his mother during training.

8. What did the club Nacional reportedly trade to Andorinha to sign a young Cristiano?

A) A set of football kits and boots

B) £1,000

C) A new team bus

D) A training pitch

9. How old was Cristiano when he left his island home to join Sporting CP's academy?

A) 10

B) 12

C) 14

D) 16

10. What city is the Sporting CP academy located in?

A) Porto

B) Braga

C) Faro

D) Lisbon

11. Why did the other boys at the academy initially laugh at Cristiano?

A) His messy hair

B) His small boots

C) His "foreign" or "country-like" accent

D) His skinny frame

12. What rule did Cristiano break at the Sporting CP academy to improve his physique?

A) He ate extra meals from the staff kitchen.

B) He sneaked out of his dorm to lift weights in the dark.

C) He played in unauthorized street tournaments.

D) He refused to attend classroom lessons.

13. What historic feat did Cristiano achieve in a single season at Sporting CP?

A) He scored 50 goals in the youth league.

B) He played for the U16, U17, U18, B-team, and senior team in one year.

C) He became the youngest captain in club history.

D) He won the Ballon d'Or as a teenager.

14. In 2003, Sporting CP played a friendly match to inaugurate their new stadium. Which team did they play?

A) Arsenal

B) Real Madrid

C) Manchester United

D) Juventus

15. Which legendary manager refused to let his team's bus leave the stadium until he signed Cristiano?

A) Arsène Wenger

B) José Mourinho

C) Carlo Ancelotti

D) Sir Alex Ferguson

16. When he arrived at Manchester United, what jersey number did Cristiano originally ask for to avoid the pressure of the #7?

A) 17

B) 28

C) 77

D) 10

17. What technique did Cristiano practice in the rain to make his free kicks wobble and dip?

A) The Rabona

B) The Trivela

C) The Knuckleball

D) The Panenka

18. Against which team did Manchester United win the 2008 UEFA Champions League Final in a rainy Moscow stadium?

A) Barcelona

B) Bayern Munich

C) Chelsea

D) AC Milan

19. How old was Cristiano when he won his very first
Ballon d'Or?

A) 21

B) 23

C) 25

D) 27

20. What was the world record transfer fee Real Madrid
paid for Cristiano in 2009?

A) £50 million

B) £80 million

C) £100 million

D) £120 million

21. What jersey number was Cristiano given when he first
arrived at Real Madrid?

A) 7

B) 9

C) 11

D) 28

22. How many Champions League titles did Cristiano win with Real Madrid between 2014 and 2018?

A) Two

B) Three

C) Four

D) Five

23. Against which team did Cristiano score his famous "impossible" bicycle kick in 2018?

A) Juventus

B) Atlético Madrid

C) Liverpool

D) Barcelona

24. In 2016, Cristiano helped Portugal win a major international trophy. What was it?

A) The FIFA World Cup

B) The UEFA Nations League

C) The UEFA European Championship (Euro 2016)

D) The Confederations Cup

25. Which Italian club did Cristiano join in 2018?

A) AC Milan

B) Inter Milan

C) AS Roma

D) Juventus

26. What nickname did they give him in Italy because of his incredible physical fitness?

A) The Machine

B) The Cyborg

C) The Gladiator

D) The Emperor

27. What Saudi Arabian club did Cristiano sign for in 2023?

A) Al-Hilal

B) Al-Ittihad

C) Al-Nassr

D) Al-Ahli

28. How many career goals is Cristiano trying to reach as his ultimate goal before retiring?

A) 800

B) 900

C) 1,000

D) 1,200

29. What is Cristiano's unique daily sleep schedule to keep his brain and muscles fresh?

A) Ten hours of straight sleep every night

B) Three hours at night and four hours during the day

C) Five 90-minute naps throughout the day

D) Sleeping only on his back in a hyperbaric chamber

30. Why does Cristiano choose not to get any tattoos?

A) He doesn't like needles.

B) So he can donate blood and bone marrow more frequently.

C) Real Madrid strictly forbid tattoos for their "Galácticos".

D) He wants to preserve his image for sponsors.

ANSWER KEY

1. A) February 5, 1985

2. B) Madeira

3. C) Gardener

4. C) The American actor and President Ronald Reagan

5. C) Abelinha (Little Bee)

6. B) Andorinha

7. C) He cried out of passion if his team lost or a teammate missed a goal.

8. A) A set of football kits and boots

9. B) 12

10. D) Lisbon

11. C) His "foreign" or "country-like" accent

12. B) He sneaked out of his dorm to lift weights in the dark.

13. B) He played for the U16, U17, U18, B-team, and senior team in one year.

14. C) Manchester United

15. D) Sir Alex Ferguson

16. B) 28

17. C) The Knuckleball

18. C) Chelsea

19. B) 23

20. B) £80 million

21. B) 9

22. C) Four

23. A) Juventus

24. C) The UEFA European Championship (Euro 2016)

25. D) Juventus

26. B) The Cyborg

27. C) Al-Nassr

28. C) 1,000

29. C) Five 90-minute naps throughout the day

30. B) So he can donate blood and bone marrow more frequently.

The CR7 Way:
Habit Tracker & Routine Builder

THE "AGUA!" CHALLENGE

Did you know that just like your body, Cristiano Ronaldo's body is about 60% water? During a famous press conference, CR7 moved two bottles of sugary soda out of the camera's view, held up a bottle of water, and told the whole world: "Agua!" (Water!).

To run fast and think clearly, your muscles and brain need to be hydrated. Real champions don't run on sugar; they run on hydration.

Your Mission:

For the next 7 days, try to swap out sugary drinks for water. Every time you drink a full glass of water, color in one of the bottles below. Can you hit your daily goal for a whole week?

Color in the bottle for each day you hit your goal!

Day1: 

Day 2:

Day3:

Day 4:

Day 5:

Day 6:

Day 7:

BUILD THE CHAMPION'S PLATE

You wouldn't put cheap dirt into a high-performance sports car like a Ferrari, right? Cristiano treats his body the same way. He eats up to six small meals a day to keep his energy high, focusing on fresh fish, grilled chicken, and lots of vegetables.

Your Mission: It's game day! In the blank space below, draw your ultimate pre-game meal. Use the "CR7 Fuel Checklist" to make sure you have everything you need to dominate the pitch.

The CR7 Fuel Checklist (Check off what you include!):

- [ ] Protein: (Chicken, fish, eggs, or beans to build strong muscles!)

- [ ] Veggies: (Broccoli, spinach, or carrots for vitamins!)

- [ ] Carbs: (Rice, sweet potatoes, or pasta for quick energy!)

- [ ] Hydration: (A big glass of agua!)

On the next page, draw or color in the plate for each day you hit your goal!

Day 1:

Day 2:

Day 3:

Day 4:

Day 5:

Day 6:

Day 7:

REST TO BE THE BEST

People talk a lot about how hard Cristiano trains, but his real secret weapon is how he recovers. He famously takes up to five 90-minute naps a day and uses ice baths to soothe his muscles. Why? Because your muscles don't get stronger while you work out—they get stronger while you *sleep*.

Your Mission: Track your sleep for the next week. Experts say kids your age need 9 to 12 hours of sleep every night to perform at their best. Are you getting enough rest to be a legend?

On the next page, draw or color in the moon for each day you hit your goal!

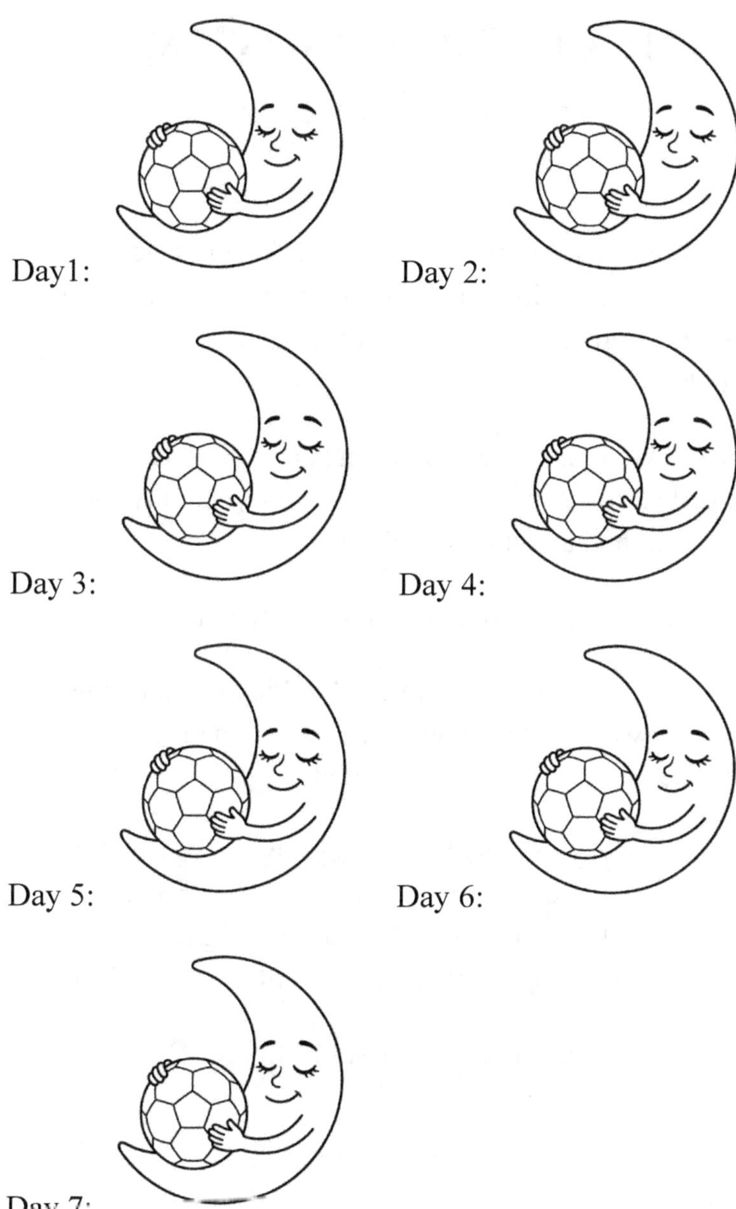

Day1:

Day 2:

Day 3:

Day 4:

Day 5:

Day 6:

Day 7:

THE CR7 TRAINING CAMP:
30 Day Challenge

Cristiano didn't become the best in the world by accident. When he was growing up on the steep, uneven streets of Madeira, he practiced the exact same basic skills every single day.

For the next 30 days, your mission is to complete these three drills. You don't need a fancy training facility—just a ball, a wall, and an elite mentality!

DRILL 1: The Madeira Wall Pass (Accuracy)

- *The Legend:* Cristiano used to kick a ball against the walls of his neighborhood, alternating feet until he was perfectly "two-footed."

- *The Drill:* Stand about 5 steps away from a sturdy wall (or ask a friend/parent to pass with you). Pass the ball against the wall with your right foot, trap the rebound, and then pass it with your left foot.

- *Your Daily Goal:* 20 passes right foot, 20 passes left foot.

DRILL 2: The Step-Over Sprint (Speed & Footwork)

- *The Legend:* To beat older, bigger kids, CR7 practiced his step-overs until his feet were a blur, completely confusing the defenders.

- *The Drill:* Place two markers (shoes or water bottles) about 10 steps apart. Dribble toward the marker, perform two quick step-overs, and sprint past it.

- *Your Daily Goal:* Do this 10 times in a row without losing control of the ball.

DRILL 3: The Hang-Time Jump (Explosive Power)

- *The Legend:* CR7 can jump almost 10 feet in the air! He built this power by focusing on explosive leg strength.

- *The Drill:* Find a safe, soft spot of grass. Crouch down and jump as high as you possibly can, bringing your knees to your chest.

- *Your Daily Goal:* 3 sets of 10 explosive jumps.

Day	Wall Passes	Speed Step	Hang Time
1			
2			
3			
4			
5			
6			
7			
8			
9			
10			
11			
12			
13			
14			
15			

Day	Wall Passes	Speed Step	Hang Time
16			
17			
18			
19			
20			
21			
22			
23			
24			
25			
26			
27			
28			
29			
30			

The "Bounce Back":
Mental Toughness Journal

From Heartbreak To Champion

Did you know that even the greatest players in the world make huge mistakes? In the 2008 Champions League Final in Moscow, the game came down to a tense penalty shootout. Cristiano stepped up to take his shot—and he missed.

He lay facedown in the pouring rain, crying because he thought he had ruined everything for his team. But his teammates rallied, they won the game, and Cristiano went from heartbreak to pure joy. He didn't let that one miss ruin his career. Instead, he used it as fuel to practice even harder.

Your Turn: Think about a time you messed up during a game, a test, or an activity. Write down what happened, and more importantly, write down what you *learned* from it so you can be better next time.

JOURNAL ENTRY 1

What happened?

____

____

____

____

____

What did I learn?

____

____

____

____

____

How did I, or how can I, use that to improve?

____

____

____

____

____

JOURNAL ENTRY 2

What happened?

____

____

____

____

What did I learn?

____

____

____

____

How did I, or how can I, use that to improve?

____

____

____

____

JOURNAL ENTRY 3

What happened?

What did I learn?

How did I, or how can I, use that to improve?

The Circle Of Control

When 12-year-old Cristiano moved to the Sporting CP academy in Lisbon, the other kids laughed at him because of his island accent. He felt like an outsider and cried every night.

Cristiano couldn't control what the other boys said about him. But he realized he *could* control how hard he worked on the training pitch. Once he started outplaying everyone, the laughing stopped. Champions focus their energy only on things they can control.

Your Mission: Look at the list of things below. Write them into the correct circle. If you can control it, put it in the inner circle. If you can't, put it in the outer circle!

- The Referee's Calls

- My Attitude After a Mistake

- The Weather During a Game

- How Hard I Try at Practice

- How Tall the Other Team Is

- Getting Enough Sleep Before Game Day

Inner the circle: Things I can control.

Outer the circle: Things I cannot control.

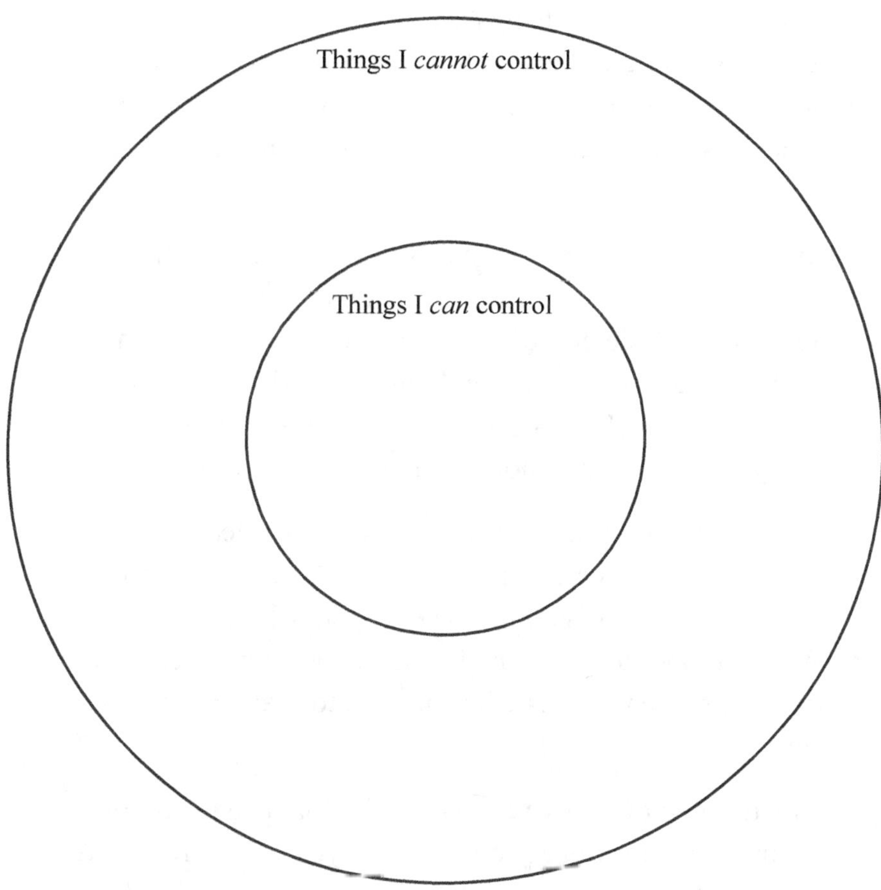

Your "Elite Mentality" Contract

When Cristiano was playing for his very first club, Andorinha, his teammates sometimes called him "Crybaby" behind his back. But Cristiano didn't cry because he was hurt or bullied. He cried out of pure passion. If he passed the ball and a teammate missed, or if his team lost a game, he would sob right there on the grass. He simply couldn't understand how anyone could be okay with losing. Even as a young boy, his standards for himself and his team were impossibly high.

Coaches know that this intense passion is actually the first sign of an "Elite Mentality". While other kids would go home and completely forget about a lost game, Cristiano would stay awake in bed, thinking about what he could do better next time. He learned early on that to be the very best, you have to care more than everyone else around you.

Later, at the Sporting CP academy, Cristiano learned another massive secret: talent is only 50% of the puzzle. The other 50% is discipline. The players who actually become professionals aren't just the ones with the coolest tricks; they are the ones who show up to practice first and leave last.

Now it's time to sign your own professional contract. Pick one big goal you want to achieve this year, and write down the three daily steps you will take to get there.

THE ELITE MENTALITY PLEDGE

I, _______________________, promise to bring 100% effort to everything I do.

My Big Goal for This Year Is:

____

To reach my goal, my 3 daily habits will be:

1. _______________________________________

2. _______________________________________

3. _______________________________________

I will not give up when things get hard.

I will not quit trying if I don't succeed at first.

I will keep a positive attitude and always remember it is a game, and games are supposed to fun!

Player Signature: _______________________

Date: _____________

100 CR7 Fast- Facts

You probably already aced the "super-fan" quiz, but there's more than just 30 things to know about CR7. Below are 100 fast facts to know (and maybe impress your friends!).

1. Cristiano was born on February 5, 1985, on the volcanic island of Madeira, Portugal.

2. His full legal name is Cristiano Ronaldo dos Santos Aveiro.

3. He was named "Ronaldo" after his father's favorite American actor, Ronald Reagan.

4. He grew up in a small, tin-roofed house in the San Antonio neighborhood of Funchal.

5. He is the youngest of four children, alongside his siblings Hugo, Elma, and Katia.

6. His father, José Dinis Aveiro, worked as a municipal gardener.

7. His mother, Maria Dolores, worked tirelessly as a cook and cleaning lady to provide for the family.

8. As a young boy, his friends nicknamed him "Abelinha" (Little Bee) because he was always buzzing around the field.

9. He also earned the nickname "Crybaby" because he would cry passionately if his team lost or a teammate missed a pass.

10. At age 15, he was diagnosed with a racing heart condition that required laser surgery to fix before he could continue his football career.

Sporting CP & The Academy

11. His first organized football club was Andorinha, where his father worked as the kit man.

12. At age 10, the island's biggest club, Nacional, signed him by trading a set of football kits and boots to Andorinha.

13. In 1997, he left his family behind to sign a contract with the Sporting CP academy in Lisbon.

14. He cried every night when he first moved to Lisbon because he missed his home and family.

15. He would sneak out of his dorm at night to lift weights in the dark because he was too young to use the gym.

16. He is the only player in Sporting CP history to play for the U16, U17, U18, B-team, and senior team in a single season.

17. He made his professional debut on October 7, 2002, at 17 years old.

18. In his league debut against Moreirense, he scored
two goals.

19. Before joining Manchester United, he actually
visited London, wore an Arsenal jersey, and nearly
signed for them.

20. In 2003, he played a friendly match against
Manchester United and dazzled the players so much
that they begged their manager to sign him.

Manchester United (First Stint)

21. He was the first-ever Portuguese player to sign for
Manchester United.

22. The club paid a record-breaking £12.24 million for
the 18-year-old.

23. He originally asked to wear the number 28 jersey,
but Sir Alex Ferguson insisted he take the legendary
number 7.

24. He made his Manchester United debut as a
substitute against Bolton Wanderers on August 16,
2003.

25. He tied weights to his ankles during training to
make his feet faster on the pitch.

26. He hired a personal chef, physiotherapist, and sleep
coach years before it was common for players to do
so.

27. He won his first UEFA Champions League title with
Manchester United in 2008 in a rainy Moscow
stadium.

28. During the penalty shootout of that 2008 final, he
actually missed his kick.

29. He scored a staggering 42 goals in all competitions
during the 2007–08 season.

30. He won his first Ballon d'Or (Golden Ball) in 2008
at the age of 23.

Real Madrid Era

31. In 2009, he transferred to Real Madrid for a world-
record fee of £80 million.

32. His stadium presentation broke a 25-year-old
attendance record with 80,000 fans packing the
Bernabéu.

33. He wore the number 9 jersey during his first season
at Real Madrid.

34. He arrived at the training ground two hours before
everyone else and left two hours after.

35. He scored 17 goals in the 2013-14 Champions
League season, the most ever in a single campaign.

36. Between 2014 and 2018, he led Real Madrid to four
Champions League titles.

37. He scored the penalty that sealed the famous "La Décima" (Real Madrid's 10th European title) in 2014.

38. He leaped nearly eight feet high to score what is considered the greatest bicycle kick in tournament history against Juventus in 2018.

39. He is the all-time leading scorer in Real Madrid history, leaving the club with 450 goals.

40. He became the first player to score in three different Champions League finals.

Juventus & The Return to Old Trafford

41. In 2018, looking for a new challenge, he moved to Italy to join Juventus.

42. He helped Juventus win two Serie A titles.

43. He became the fastest player in Juventus history to reach 100 goals for the club.

44. Fans in Italy nicknamed him "The Cyborg" because his physical fitness seemed unbreakable.

45. In 2021, he shocked the world by returning to Manchester United.

46. He scored two goals in his very first game back at Old Trafford.

47. During his second stint at United, he scored his 800th career top-level goal, the first male player to ever do so.

48. He scored hat-tricks against Tottenham and Norwich City during his return season.

49. He won the Premier League Player of the Month in April 2022.

50. He mutually parted ways with Manchester United just before the 2022 World Cup.

Al-Nassr & Saudi Arabia

51. In 2023, he signed for Al-Nassr in Riyadh, Saudi Arabia.

52. His contract with Al-Nassr is widely reported to make him the highest-paid athlete in the world.

53. He sparked a massive global movement, leading superstars like Neymar and Karim Benzema to follow him to the Saudi Pro League.

54. He became the Saudi Pro League's top scorer.

55. He scored 54 total goals in 2023, making him the world's top goalscorer for that calendar year.

56. He won his first trophy with Al-Nassr in the 2023 Arab Club Champions Cup.

57. He frequently scores hat-tricks in the Saudi Pro League, continuing to build his record-breaking tally.

58. In early 2026, he crossed the 950-goal mark.

59. His ultimate professional mission is to reach 1,000 career goals.

60. His famous "Siuuu!" celebration is passionately yelled by fans at every Al-Nassr home game.

International Dominance (Portugal)

61. He made his senior international debut for Portugal in 2003 against Kazakhstan.

62. He scored his first major tournament goal at Euro 2004 when he was a teenager.

63. He won his first major international trophy at the UEFA European Championship in 2016.

64. During the Euro 2016 Final, he was taken off on a stretcher due to a painful knee injury.

65. Refusing to quit, he spent the rest of the 2016 Final acting as a second coach, screaming instructions from the sidelines.

66. He holds the world record for the most international goals scored by a male player (over 130).

67. He is the most-capped male player in the history of international football.

68. He led Portugal to victory in the inaugural UEFA Nations League in 2019.

69. He is the only male player in history to score in five different World Cup tournaments.

70. He plans to continue leading his country and has stated his desire to play in the 2026 World Cup in North America.

Physical Prowess & Training Habits

71. He eats up to six small meals a day consisting of fish, chicken, and fresh vegetables.

72. He strictly drinks water and refuses to consume sugary sodas.

73. He went viral for moving two Coca-Cola bottles away at a press conference and holding up a water bottle.

74. Instead of sleeping eight straight hours, he often takes five 90-minute naps throughout the day.

75. He installed a cryotherapy chamber in his house to freeze his muscles for faster recovery.

76. He takes an ice-cold bath after every game to reduce swelling.

77. He focuses heavily on explosive training, doing 1,000+ ab crunches in a single week.

78. He used to practice passing against a neighborhood wall endlessly to become perfectly two-footed.

79. He practiced his step-over skill thousands of times until he could perform it at high speeds.

80. He is famous for his "knuckleball" free-kick technique, which makes the ball wobble in the air.

Records & Accolades

81. He has won the Ballon d'Or five times.

82. He has won five total UEFA Champions League titles (one with Manchester United, four with Real Madrid).

83. He is the all-time leading goalscorer in the UEFA Champions League with over 140 goals.

84. He has won 4 European Golden Shoes, given to the leading goalscorer in league matches from the top division of every European national league.

85. He and Lionel Messi are considered the greatest modern rivals in sports history, sharing a decade of Ballon d'Or awards.

86. He won the FIFA Puskás Award for the most aesthetically significant, or "most beautiful", goal of the year in 2009.

87. The acronym "CR7" comes from his initials and his legendary number 7 jersey.

88. He holds the record for the most goals scored in the Real Madrid versus Barcelona "El Clásico" rivalry alongside Alfredo Di Stéfano.

89. He has won domestic league titles in England, Spain, and Italy.

90. He is actively the highest-scoring male professional footballer in recorded history.

Off the Pitch (Business, Charity & Lifestyle)

91. He was the first person in history to ever reach 600 million followers on Instagram.

92. He has more social media followers than the entire population of North America combined.

93. He does not have a single tattoo, choosing to stay ink-free so he can frequently donate blood and bone marrow.

94. He has an entire museum dedicated to himself, the Museu CR7, in his hometown of Funchal.

95. There is an international airport in Madeira named the Cristiano Ronaldo International Airport.

96. Astronomers named a galaxy "Cosmos Redshift 7" (CR7) inspired by him.

97. He has a massive business empire including CR7-branded hotels, underwear, fragrances, and fitness centers.

98. He sold his 2013 Ballon d'Or replica trophy at a
charity auction for €600,000 to benefit the Make-A-
Wish Foundation.

99. He has four children (Cristiano Jr., twins Eva and
Mateo, and Alana Martina) and shares a daughter
(Bella) with his partner Georgina Rodríguez.

100.   He famously stated, "I don't follow the
records, the records follow me.".

FINAL COACH'S TIP:

You don't have to be the best player on the team today.

You just have to be a little bit better than *you* were yesterday.

<u>That is the "CR7 Way."</u>